D0394211

NO LONGER PROPERTY OF
SEATTLE PUBLIC LIBRARY

GAME DAY
FOOD

MAD HUNGRY

GAME DAY FOOD

Fan-Favorite Recipes for Winning
Dips, Nachos, Wings & Drinks

LUCINDA SCALA QUINN

Artisan | New York

CONTENTS

Drinks 98

INTRODUCTION

We all love the idea of sitting down to watch a game with a big plate of homemade fried chicken, a cup of bubbling chili, maybe even some artichoke dip and crudités. But too often we find ourselves settling for delivery pizza, frozen chicken nuggets, and packaged mac 'n' cheese. Even when you're watching the action from the sidelines, these foods are no way to nourish a body. It's true that when it's time to cheer on the team, most of us don't gravitate toward raw salads or grain bowls, but that doesn't mean you can't enjoy healthier versions of the foods you crave for the tailgate or the Super Bowl party. The answer to solving this dilemma, as is often the case, is to make your game day fare at home.

We've reached an imbalance: we spend more money to eat inferior food out, and in the process, we not only jeopardize our health but also deprive ourselves of less expensive, tastier, and more nutritious home-cooked meals. And there is no healthier diet than fresh food— vegetables, fruits, whole grains, meat, poultry, and seafood—eaten in moderation. Home cooking allows you to skip high cost and poor nutrition by using real ingredients and smart cooking techniques.

Roll up your sleeves and get into the kitchen. You can produce all those fan-favorite foods right now! This book shows how you can make all the dishes you enjoy eating when the game is on at home or when you're tailgating outdoors. So leave the waxy, artificially flavored, preservative-laden dips from the back shelf of the grocery store behind for new staples like homemade Queso Fundido (page 14) and Caramelized Onion and Bacon Dip (page 17). We all love the loaded potato skins at the local sports bar and the baby back ribs from our favorite barbecue spot, but you can learn to make those, too (see page 28 and page 84). Capture the alluring flavors of your favorite Asian take-out restaurant with easy-to-make Potsticker Dumplings (page 22) or Crunchy Sesame Chicken Wings (page 27). Maybe you're adventurous and want to try some Jerk Chicken and Mango Chutney Sandwiches (page 68), or you go for a Classic French Dip (page 64), or you simply simmer a big pot of comforting Chili (page 90). But cook what you crave at home! Excavate your own taste memories and assemble that personal recipe box. Restore your food traditions and make new ones. Reclaim your home kitchen and make game day eating something special every time.

SNACKS

basic salsa

makes 2 cups (512 g)

This quick salsa can be used as a dip for tortilla chips or as a topping for eggs, tacos, chicken, or fish. It will keep in the refrigerator for a few days.

2 large tomatoes, cored and finely chopped

4 small radishes, halved and finely sliced

1 to 2 serrano or jalapeño chiles, sliced

⅓ cup (40 g) finely chopped white onion

2 tablespoons chopped fresh cilantro

1 teaspoon coarse salt

½ cup (120 mL) water

Combine all the ingredients in a medium bowl. Serve at room temperature or chilled.

salsa verde

makes 2 cups (512 g)

12 whole tomatillos

½ white onion, coarsely chopped

2 garlic cloves, peeled

2 serrano or jalapeño chiles, stems removed

2 teaspoons salt

Peel the tomatillos and simmer in water for 5 minutes. Drain and roughly pulse with a blender or food processor with all the other ingredients until smooth, adding water as necessary for desired consistency.

queso fundido

serves 2

There are few things more divinely swoonworthy than this concoction, which should almost be labeled an illegal substance. Queso fundido is insanely easy to replicate at home, and you'll be spared any cleanup hassle, because every last bit of the crispy cheese that crusts up at the bottom of the pan will be scraped up and devoured. Serve with tortillas and salsa (see page 13).

4 ounces (113 g) smoked chorizo, cut into ¼-inch (6 mm) pieces

½ small yellow onion, finely chopped

2¾ cups (12 ounces/340 g) shredded Monterey Jack cheese

8 (6-inch/15 cm) corn tortillas, warmed over a flame (see Note)

Preheat the broiler. Cook the chorizo in a 6-inch (15 cm) ovenproof skillet over medium heat until the fat begins to render, about 2 minutes. Add the onions and cook, stirring occasionally, until they soften and become translucent, about 3 minutes. Stir in the cheese.

Transfer the skillet to the broiler and broil until the cheese is bubbly and golden brown in places, 2 minutes. Serve immediately, with the tortillas.

NOTE

To get a nice charred flavor, toast the tortillas and stack them to steam and become pliable for use. Toast them one at a time, on a direct flame or in a hot skillet or *comal* (a smooth, flat Mexican griddle), until the edges start to darken, about 1 minute; flip and toast for another minute (some will puff up once you flip them). If they seem too toasted, almost crisp, stack them on top of one another wrapped in a cloth. To keep them fresh for 30 minutes, wrap the cloth stack in foil and keep in a warm place.

caramelized onion and bacon dip

makes 2 cups (480 g)

If you love—yet hate—that packaged onion-soup-mix dip, this is the recipe for you. It is a richer, deeper-flavored, cleaner-ingredient excuse for a potato-chip-dipping marathon. Or smear it over flatbreads for a classier affair. The dip can be refrigerated for up to 3 days.

¼ cup (60 mL) extra-virgin olive oil

3 pounds (1.3 kg) yellow onions, halved lengthwise and thinly sliced, crosswise

1 teaspoon coarse salt

2 tablespoons white wine vinegar

5 ounces (150 g) bacon, chopped

1½ cups (215 g) mayonnaise

1 cup (242 g) sour cream

¼ cup (60 mL) safflower oil (optional, for garnish)

3 shallots, thinly sliced into rings (optional, for garnish)

Heat a large skillet. Add the olive oil. When it shimmers, add the onions and salt and cook over low heat, stirring occasionally, until the onions are deep golden in color, 45 minutes to 1 hour; add a little water if needed to prevent sticking. Add the vinegar during the last minute of cooking. Let cool.

Meanwhile, cook the bacon in a small skillet until it has rendered its fat. Using a slotted spoon, transfer the bacon to a paper towel–lined plate; reserve the fat in the pan if you will be frying the shallots. Let the bacon cool.

Stir together the mayonnaise, sour cream, onions, and bacon in a large bowl.

For the optional garnish, add the vegetable oil to the skillet with the bacon fat and heat over medium-high heat until the oil shimmers. Add the shallots, lower the heat, and cook, stirring occasionally, until golden brown, about 2 minutes. Drain the shallots on a paper towel–lined plate.

Garnish the dip with the fried shallots, if using, and serve.

guacamole

makes 2 cups (480 g)

Why buy guacamole when the homemade version simply requires mashing up a few items? There are many riffs on guacamole these days, with various vegetables, fruits, or smoked chorizo added to personalize and differentiate them, but this old-school version is a classic that will please any crowd and pair well with a variety of dishes. *Pictured on page 30.*

¼ cup (30 g) finely chopped white onion

2 serrano chiles, minced
(about 2 tablespoons)

3 tablespoons chopped fresh cilantro

1 teaspoon coarse salt

3 ripe Hass avocados, halved, pitted, and flesh scooped out of skin

1 small tomato, chopped

Tortilla chips, warm tortillas, or flautas (see page 29), for serving

Mix together the onion, chiles, 2 tablespoons of cilantro, and the salt in a large bowl. Using a large fork, crush the avocados into the onion mixture, leaving the mixture somewhat chunky. Fold in the tomatoes. Sprinkle the remaining tablespoon of cilantro over the mixture.

Serve with tortilla chips, warm tortillas, or flautas.

cheesy corn snack

makes 4 quarts (4 L)

Many commercial versions of this snack are on the market, but this homemade version, which has all the attractive elements of the store-bought and none of the toxins (just simple flavors made with fresh ingredients), is absolutely delicious. Two hungry snackers can easily devour this batch, but it will feed up to six people for a small snack. This recipe appeals to all ages. You can intensify it with ground pepper or other desired flavoring.

2 tablespoons vegetable oil

¾ cup (160 g) popping-corn kernels

4 tablespoons (½ stick/57 g) unsalted butter, melted

⅓ cup (40 g) grated Parmesan cheese

½ teaspoon coarse salt

Heat a 4-quart (4 L) pot with a tight-fitting lid on the stovetop. Add the oil and swirl it around to coat the bottom of the pot. Get it hot enough to sizzle when a kernel hits the oil. Pour the corn in all at once, cover, and shake. Swirl the pot over the top of the burner once or twice, until you hear the first few kernels pop. Once the corn is popping, swirl the pot continuously until the popping stops. Or, use a popcorn maker if you want to. Dump the popcorn into a large bowl.

Pour the melted butter over the corn and toss well to fully coat the kernels. Sprinkle the cheese and salt over the corn and toss until everything is well combined.

baked potato poppers

makes 24 poppers; serves 6

Baked rather than deep-fried, these potato poppers are perfectly crispy on the outside and meltingly soft on the inside. They will fool even the most die-hard tater tot fiend. Panko bread crumbs are essential to the dish's success, providing the crispiest crunch.

2 large russet (baking) potatoes (about 1 pound/454 g)
½ cup (65 g) all-purpose flour
1 tablespoon cornstarch
½ teaspoon coarse salt
¼ teaspoon white pepper
1 large egg yolk
1½ cups (120 g) panko bread crumbs
¼ cup (60 mL) extra-virgin olive oil
Ketchup

Preheat the oven to 425°F (220°C), with a rack in the center position. Put a rimmed baking sheet in the oven to preheat. Peel and grate the potatoes and transfer to a large bowl. Cover with boiling water by two inches. Let stand for 10 minutes.

Drain the potatoes in a colander and rinse thoroughly with cold water. Squeeze the potatoes to remove excess moisture and transfer back to the large bowl. Add the flour, cornstarch, salt, pepper, and egg yolk and fold into the potatoes.

Spread the panko on another rimmed baking sheet. With wet hands, pinch off tablespoons of the potato mixture, form into balls, and coat with the panko crumbs.

Carefully remove the hot baking sheet from the oven and coat with 2 tablespoons of the olive oil. Quickly transfer the poppers to the baking sheet and drizzle with the remaining 2 tablespoons olive oil. Bake for about 30 minutes, flipping once, until golden brown and crispy. Serve with ketchup.

potsticker dumplings

makes 36 dumplings

Like most things wrapped in dough, this is a friendly, go-to choice. The variations on dumpling fillings and shapes are endless, and it is surprising how easy these are to make at home. Start with a large batch, freeze it, and you'll always have a quick snack, appetizer, or meal ready in about 8 minutes. Dumpling wrappers—Chinese wonton or Japanese gyoza skins are the same thing—are now widely available in the produce or frozen-food sections of most markets.

SOY-VINEGAR DIPPING SAUCE

½ cup (120 mL) soy sauce

1 teaspoon rice vinegar

½ teaspoon toasted sesame oil

2 teaspoons sugar

1 whole scallion, trimmed and sliced

1 hot green chile, thinly sliced

2 tablespoons water

DUMPLINGS

½ pound (8 ounces/227 g) ground turkey, chicken, or pork (if using poultry, add 1 teaspoon peanut oil to the mixture)

1 cup (127 g) finely chopped bok choy

½ teaspoon minced peeled fresh ginger

1 small garlic clove, minced

1 teaspoon soy sauce

½ teaspoon sesame oil

½ teaspoon coarse salt

1 large egg white

36 dumpling wrappers

Peanut oil, for frying

In a small bowl, combine all the ingredients for the dipping sauce. Set aside.

In a medium bowl, mix together the protein, bok choy, ginger, garlic, soy sauce, sesame oil, and salt. Stir in the egg white.

Working with six at a time, lay down the dumpling wrappers on a work surface. Spoon 1 teaspoon of filling onto each one. Lightly wet the edge of each wrapper with water. Fold the dough over and pinch around the edges. This is easiest done by picking up each dumpling and pinching around the edges with thumb and forefinger. Place on a baking sheet and cover with plastic wrap to keep the dumplings from drying out. Repeat until all filling is used. (Freeze any dumplings that will not be cooked immediately. Freeze dumplings on the wrapped tray. After they are frozen, transfer them to resealable plastic bags or wrap in plastic.)

To cook the dumplings, heat a large skillet and swirl some oil around to coat the pan. Add a single layer of potstickers. Cook for 2 to 3 minutes (2 minutes longer if frozen), until they begin to turn golden on the underside. Don't move them. Add ¼ cup (60 mL) of water to the pan and cover immediately. Cook for 5 more minutes, or until the meat is cooked through and the dumplings release from the pan. Serve immediately with the dipping sauce.

teriyaki-glazed wings

serves 4 normal people or 2 college students

Hot wings, garlic wings, honey-mustard wings, barbecue wings, and teriyaki wings are being scarfed down all over the country. Analyze your favorite take-out tastes and replicate the flavors at home using the basic cook time given here. For a straight-up collegiate-style chow-down, serve with Loaded Potato Skins (page 28).

GLAZE

⅔ cup (160 mL) low-sodium soy sauce

1⅓ cups (315 mL) sake or dry white wine

¼ cup (60 mL) mirin

One 1-inch piece ginger, peeled and minced

2 garlic cloves, minced

2 tablespoons sugar

2 pounds (907 g) whole chicken wings

1 tablespoon vegetable oil

½ teaspoon coarse salt

Preheat the oven to 375°F (190°C) with a rack in the center position. For the glaze, combine the soy sauce, sake, mirin, ginger, garlic, and sugar in a small saucepan and boil until reduced to ½ cup (120 mL), about 15 minutes. Transfer to a bowl and let cool to room temperature.

Toss the wings with the oil and salt in a bowl and transfer to a rimmed baking sheet. Bake for 30 minutes, then brush generously with the glaze. Bake for 15 minutes, basting and turning every 5 minutes until the wings look caramelized.

crunchy sesame chicken wings

makes 20 wings

Chicken wings are classic game day fare, but try these crispy Asian-inspired wings for an interesting twist on a fan-favorite dish. The wings can be separated in two for smaller portions, detaching the drumette at the joint. Serve with a bottle of hot sauce at the table.

Vegetable oil, for coating the pan

20 chicken wings

3 large eggs, beaten

½ cup (70 g) sesame seeds

½ cup (65 g) all-purpose flour

2 teaspoons coarse salt

¼ teaspoon cayenne pepper

½ cup (22 g) fresh bread crumbs

2 to 3 garlic cloves, minced

Hot sauce, for serving

Preheat the oven to 375°F (190°C). Line a large rimmed baking sheet with baking parchment or coat the pan with oil. Place the chicken wings in a large bowl. Add the eggs and toss to coat.

In a small bowl, combine the sesame seeds, flour, salt, cayenne, bread crumbs, and garlic. Dip each wing in the sesame mixture to fully coat. Place the coated wings side by side on the prepared baking sheet.

Bake for 30 minutes and increase the temperature to 400°F (200°C). Cook until the wings are golden brown and sizzling, 20 to 30 more minutes. Immediately remove the wings from the baking sheet while hot. Serve with hot sauce.

loaded potato skins

makes 12 potato skins

Familiar foods that make us happy transport us back to our earliest tastes of deliciousness: memories often associated with pleasure and peace. With indulgent ingredients like potatoes, cheese, and bacon, these classic potato skins are substantial enough to be just as filling as they are comforting.

6 large russet (baking) potatoes (about 3½ pounds/1.6 kg), scrubbed

6 slices bacon

⅓ cup (80 mL) extra-virgin olive oil

1 teaspoon coarse salt

¼ teaspoon white pepper

1 cup (4 ounces/113 g) shredded sharp white cheddar cheese

1 cup (4 ounces/113 g) shredded Monterey Jack cheese

1 cup (242 g) sour cream

¼ cup (14 g) chopped fresh chives

Preheat the oven to 375°F (190°C) with a rack in the center position. Prick each potato several times with a fork and bake for about 1 hour, until the potatoes can be easily pierced with a toothpick. Remove from the oven and raise the oven temperature to 450°F (230°C).

Meanwhile, cook the bacon in a large skillet until crisp. Transfer to a paper towel–lined plate to drain. Chop the bacon and set aside.

When the potatoes are cool enough to handle, halve them lengthwise and scoop out most of the flesh, leaving a ¼-inch-thick (6 mm) layer of flesh attached to the skins. Reserve the scooped flesh for another use, such as mashed potatoes.

Brush the skins with the olive oil and season with the salt and pepper. Place skin-side down on a rimmed baking sheet and bake for 18 to 20 minutes, until crisp and golden.

Scatter the cheeses and bacon over the skins and bake for 5 minutes more, until the cheese is melted and bubbly. Dollop with the sour cream and chives and serve.

fake-out flautas

makes 12 flautas; serves 6

Flautas are those addictive deep-fried skinny tacos you probably see at your local taqueria. I call these flautas "fake-out" because unlike their messy, deep-fried cousins, they are a quick low-fat, baked, vegetarian gem of a recipe. Serve with Guacamole (page 18), the ultimate scoopable flavor bomb.

12 corn tortillas

1½ cups (6 ounces/170 g) grated Monterey Jack cheese

2 tomatoes, chopped

1 (15-ounce/425 g) can black beans, drained and rinsed

½ teaspoon coarse salt

Juice of ½ lime

1 tablespoon safflower or other vegetable oil

Preheat the oven to 425°F (200°C) with the racks in the upper- and lower-third positions. Lay out the tortillas on 2 rimmed baking sheets and scatter the cheese over them. Place in the oven for 1 to 2 minutes to melt the cheese.

Meanwhile, toss the tomatoes, black beans, salt, and lime juice together in a bowl.

Distribute the bean mixture evenly over the melted cheese and roll up the tortillas. Arrange side by side, seam-side down, on one baking sheet. Brush the oil over the tops. Bake for 8 minutes, or until golden and crispy.

OVEN-FRYING VERSUS DEEP-FRYING

Any deep-fried food, such as these flautas or Baked Potato Poppers (page 20), that can be reasonably replicated by oven-frying is worth a try. Oven-frying is easier to do and doesn't require the careful handling that deep-frying does. Here are a few tips:

- Coat the food with items that create a wowie crunch like panko bread crumbs or crushed tortilla chips.

- Brush a light coating of oil to coat the surface of the food before putting it in the oven.

- Preheat your metal baking pan in the oven before the food is added; this will help you achieve that audible sizzle-sear right off the bat.

- Broil for the last few minutes of cooking to finish with a golden touch.

mexican corn on the cob

serves 4

Also known as *elote*, this hot piece of corn on the cob slathered in spiced cream, cheese, and fresh lime is a popular Mexican street food. Heat the corn over a grill or use a cast-iron pan for an indoor-friendly cooking experience.

4 ears corn, in the husk

1 lime

½ cup (121 g) Mexican crema or sour cream

2 tablespoons chopped fresh cilantro

¾ cup (4 ounces/113 g) queso fresco, crumbled

⅛ teaspoon chipotle chili powder

Preheat a double-burner cast-iron grill pan over high heat (or prepare a grill). Peel the husks away from the cobs, leaving them attached. Cut 4 thin strips from a soft, inner husk and use them to tie the husks over the stalks. Remove the silk from the corn and rinse the husks under cold water to prevent them from burning when grilled.

Grate the zest from the lime and cut the lime into wedges. Stir together the crema, cilantro, and lime zest in a small bowl.

Grill the corn, turning occasionally, until the kernels are blackened in spots, about 5 minutes. Remove from the grill pan and slather with the crema mixture. Transfer to a serving platter and sprinkle the queso fresco and chili powder evenly over the corn. Garnish the platter with the lime wedges and serve immediately.

street-corner pretzels

Throughout New York City, you can find vendors selling big, fluffy, salty, doughy pretzels. The key to replicating this New York specialty is boiling and then baking the pretzels. When you drain the boiled pretzels on wire racks, don't let too much time elapse before baking, or the pretzels will deflate. The ideal baked pretzel is soft inside with a thin, golden outside layer that is firm and slightly crunchy. One pound (454 g) store-bought bread dough can be used in place of the homemade.

1 cup (240 mL) warm water

2 teaspoons sugar

¼ teaspoon coarse salt

1¼-ounce package (2¼ teaspoons/7 g) active dry yeast

3 cups (390 g) all-purpose flour, plus more for dusting

2 tablespoons unsalted butter, at room temperature

3 tablespoons baking soda

2 tablespoons pretzel salt or coarse salt

Mustard, to taste

Combine the water, sugar, salt, and yeast in a small bowl and let stand for about 5 minutes to dissolve the yeast.

Put the flour in a large bowl. Using a pastry cutter or your fingers, cut the butter into the flour until the mixture resembles coarse crumbs. Slowly pour in the yeast mixture, stirring to combine. Using your hands, gather the dough together, turn it out onto a lightly floured surface, and knead until it is no longer sticky, about 5 minutes. Cover with plastic and let rise for 30 minutes.

Cut the dough into 12 pieces. One at a time, roll each one into an 18-inch-long (46 cm) rope. Form a U shape and twist the ends together twice. Fold the twisted portion

backward over the center of the U shape to form a circle, then gently press the ends of the rope onto the dough to seal. Transfer to an oiled baking sheet (you will probably need two). Let rise for 20 minutes.

Preheat the oven to 475°F (250°C) with a rack in the center position. Bring a large pot of water to a boil and add the baking soda.

Boil the pretzels in batches, without crowding them, until puffed and slightly shiny, 1 to 2 minutes per side. Transfer to wire racks to drain.

Return the pretzels to the baking sheet and sprinkle with the pretzel salt. Bake for about 15 minutes, until golden brown and puffed up; the pretzels will keep, uncovered, at room temperature for up to 12 hours. Rewarm in a 250°F (120°C) oven if desired and serve with your favorite mustard.

chicken and black bean nachos

serves 6 to 8

Nachos can stand an ingredient riff, but to make sure that the cheese is melted throughout and that each bite has the requisite combination of tastes and textures, follow this plan.

2 tablespoons safflower oil

1 small white onion, chopped

1 (15-ounce/425 g) can black beans, drained and rinsed

½ teaspoon ground cumin

¼ teaspoon dried oregano

Coarse salt and freshly ground black pepper

12 ounces (340 g) tortilla chips

2 cups (250 g) shredded cooked chicken

1⅔ cups (10 ounces/284 g) shredded Monterey Jack cheese

1¾ cups (16 ounces/454 g) salsa, store-bought or Salsa Verde (see page 13)

1 avocado, pitted, peeled, and coarsely chopped

1 jalapeño, thinly sliced

Sour cream, for serving

Preheat the oven to 350°F (180°C) with the rack in the center position. Heat the safflower oil in a 10-inch (25 cm) skillet over medium-high heat. Add the onions and sauté until translucent, about 3 minutes. Add the black beans, cumin, and oregano. Season to taste with salt and pepper. Remove from the heat.

Arrange one-third of the tortilla chips on a baking sheet or oven-safe platter. Top with one-third each of the black beans, chicken, cheese, and salsa. Repeat this layering twice more. Transfer to the oven and bake until the cheese is melted throughout, 18 to 20 minutes. Remove from the oven and top with the avocado, jalapeño, and dollops of sour cream. Serve immediately.

hamjam cheddar puffs

makes 18 pieces

These savory-sweet treats are an any-meal, anytime choice. Add these puffs to your repertoire so you'll be just as prepared for a morning game as one in the evening. The full flavors of the mustard and sharp cheddar cheese set off the sweet berry jam in a deliciously savory way.

1 sheet puff pastry, thawed according to package instructions

2 tablespoons Dijon mustard

¾ cup (3 ounces/85 g) shredded sharp cheddar cheese

¼ teaspoon freshly ground black pepper

4 to 5 ounces (113 to 142 g) ham, cut into 18 matchsticks (about ¼ inch/5 mm wide by 3 inches/8 cm long)

⅓ cup (100 g) favorite jam

1 large egg

Preheat the oven to 425°F (220°C) with the rack in the center position. Line a baking sheet with parchment paper, foil, or a silicone-rubber baking pad.

Roll out the puff pastry to a 12-inch (30 cm) square. Brush the mustard over the entire surface of the pastry and sprinkle with the cheese and pepper. Cut the dough into thirds and then into thirds again to make 9 squares. Cut each square in half diagonally to make 18 triangles.

Place a piece of ham on the lower third of each triangle, add a small spoonful of jam, and roll up. Place each bundle seam-side down on the lined baking sheet. Whisk together the egg and 1 teaspoon water in a small bowl. Brush each bundle with egg wash and bake until golden brown, 16 to 18 minutes. Serve immediately.

neo clams casino

serves 6 to 8 as an appetizer

This updated classic lets the clam flavor shine through with fewer crumbs and doubles the usual amounts of parsley and lemon zest for a much fresher taste.

2 dozen clams, preferably littlenecks

¼ cup (30 g) bread crumbs

¼ cup (10 g) chopped fresh parsley leaves

3 garlic cloves, minced

2 strips bacon or sliced pancetta, cooked and crumbled

Finely grated zest and juice of 1 lemon

½ teaspoon crushed red pepper flakes

Coarse salt

Extra-virgin olive oil

Place the clams in a large pot with a tight-fitting lid and add ¼ inch (6 mm) of water to the pot. Steam until the shells open, about 6 minutes. With a slotted spoon or ladle, lift the clams out of the pot, remove and discard one half of the shell on each clam, leaving the meat attached to the other (if the meat falls out during steaming, place it in an empty shell). Arrange the clams side by side in a baking dish.

Preheat the broiler and set the oven rack at least 4 inches (10 cm) from it. Combine the bread crumbs, parsley, garlic, bacon, lemon zest and juice, red pepper flakes, and a pinch of salt. Top each clam with a teaspoon of the bread crumb mixture and drizzle oil over the top. Broil until the mixture is bubbling and golden brown, about 3 minutes. Watch carefully as the bread crumbs will easily burn. Serve immediately.

broccoli francese

serves 4 to 6

Cheesy eggs surround and infuse these green florets with a rich flavor that anyone can get behind. You can also include asparagus or spinach for an equally delicious result.

1 head broccoli, separated into small florets, stem peeled and thinly sliced into coins

6 large eggs

¾ cup (85 g) grated Parmesan or Romano cheese, plus more for serving

Coarse salt and freshly ground black pepper

2 teaspoons extra-virgin olive oil

1 lemon, cut into wedges, for serving

Bring ½ inch (1 cm) of water to a boil in a 3-quart (3 L) saucepan. Add the broccoli, cover, and steam until crisp but tender, 3 to 4 minutes. Drain. In a bowl, whisk together the eggs, cheese, a pinch of salt, and a couple grinds of pepper.

Heat a medium nonstick or well-seasoned cast-iron skillet over high heat. Swirl in the oil. When it shimmers, scatter the cooked broccoli over the bottom of the skillet. Pour the egg mixture over the broccoli and swirl the skillet to cover the bottom of the pan. Cook until golden on the bottom, about 3 minutes. Flip and cook until the eggs are set, 3 to 4 minutes more. (It should flip easily, but if you prefer, place a plate slightly larger than the skillet on top of the pan and turn the "pancake" over onto it, cooked side up. Then slide it back into the pan.)

Slide the cooked eggs onto a cutting board and cut into bite-size pieces for snacking or appetizers, or into wedges to serve as a side dish. Sprinkle with a dusting of cheese and serve with lemon wedges. This can be eaten warm or at room temperature.

MAINS

soccer breakfast

serves 4 to 6

This "full English" (minus the blood sausage) is a cooking sprint that is worth it. Have all your prep done so you can start cooking about 30 minutes before kickoff, and you'll be sitting down with everyone else eating a hot meal when the game starts.

8 pork sausage links, aka "bangers"

8 ounces (227 g) sliced bacon

1½ tablespoons unsalted butter, plus more for toast

1 onion, cut into ¼-inch-thick (6 mm) slices

4 small plum tomatoes, halved lengthwise, or 2 large tomatoes, sliced ½ inch (1 cm) thick

8 ounces (227 g) mushrooms, cleaned and halved, or sliced if large

1 (13½-ounce/390 g) can Heinz beans in tomato sauce, or similar Brit-style beans in red sauce

6 large eggs

Coarse salt and freshly ground black pepper

6 slices bread, toasted

Place the sausages and bacon in a large skillet over high heat. Cook through until golden brown, turning a couple of times, 10 to 15 minutes. Transfer to a paper towel–lined plate to drain, and keep hot in a warm oven.

Pour off most of the fat from the pan, then add 1 tablespoon of the butter and melt over medium-high heat. Add the onions, tomatoes, and mushrooms so they lie in a single layer and cook, turning once, until cooked through, with golden-brown edges in spots, 4 to 5 minutes per side. (Cook in batches or use two pans.) Transfer the vegetables to a plate and keep hot in a warm oven. (If your pan is large enough, push the vegetables to one side and cook the eggs on the other.)

continued

Place the beans in a small pot over medium heat. Place the bread in the toaster. Put your serving plates in the warm oven.

Add the remaining ½ tablespoon butter to the skillet and swirl it to coat. Immediately crack the eggs into the skillet. Add 1 teaspoon water to the pan, reduce the heat to medium-low, cover, and cook until the whites are set, about 2 minutes.

Place an egg or two on each warm plate. Add a couple of pieces of bacon, a sausage or two, a piece of tomato, some onions, a few mushrooms, and a spoonful of beans. Season with salt and pepper. Butter the toast and serve.

savory chicken pocket pies

makes 10 pocket pies

These handheld pies are just as fun to prepare as they are convenient to enjoy. Avoid any pregame stress by preparing these pocket pies in advance and freezing them until game day, when you can simply pop them in the oven half an hour before the game.

FILLING

1 (3-pound/1.3 kg) chicken
(to get 1 heaping cup/150 g of
shredded meat; you can freeze
remainder for other recipes)

2 tablespoons unsalted butter

½ cup (60 g) chopped onion

⅓ cup (40 g) chopped celery
 (1 large stalk)

⅓ cup (43 g) chopped carrot (1 carrot)

½ teaspoon coarse salt

2 tablespoons all-purpose flour

1½ cups (360 mL) chicken broth (from
the reduced poaching liquid)

¼ cup (30 g) grated Parmesan cheese

1 recipe (2 disks) Cream Cheese Pastry
(recipe follows)

1 large egg, for egg wash

Place the chicken in a pot and add water to barely cover. Bring to a boil, reduce the heat, and simmer for 50 minutes. Skim and discard any foam as it rises to the surface. Remove the chicken to cool. Continue to boil the broth to reduce and concentrate to about 4 cups (1 L). Remove the meat from the chicken and shred.

To make the filling, melt the butter in a medium-size hot skillet and add the onion, celery, and carrot. Sauté over medium heat for 2 to 3 minutes. Stir in the salt and flour and cook for 1 minute more. Add the chicken broth and stir until thickened, about 2 minutes. Stir in 1 heaping cup (150 g) shredded chicken and the Parmesan cheese. Cool in the fridge.

continued

Preheat the oven to 375°F (190°C). Butter or line a baking sheet.

To form the pocket pies, work with half a disk of dough at a time, rolling it out on a floured surface. Using an overturned bowl (about 5 inches/13 cm across), cut out circles about 3 at a time from each piece of dough. After cutting out all your circles, gather all dough scraps, reroll, and cut out a final time. Place ¼ cup filling on one side of a dough circle. Wet the edges of the dough with water. Fold the dough over to form a half-circle. Pinch the edges of the dough together. Crimp the edges with a fork. Repeat the process until all the filling is used. The pocket pies can be frozen at this point.

Place the pocket pies on the prepared baking sheet and chill for a few minutes. Prick each pie on top twice with a fork. When ready to bake, beat the egg with 1 tablespoon water. Brush the egg wash over each pocket pie. Bake for 20 to 25 minutes, until golden brown. Let rest for 5 minutes before serving. The pies can be cooled and frozen to reheat in the microwave.

FREEZING AND BAKING POCKET PIES

Place freshly prepared pies in a single layer on a baking sheet and put in the freezer. Once they are frozen solid, they can be stacked together in a resealable bag or wrapped in plastic for easy storage. To bake from frozen, place on a baking sheet, brush with egg wash, and bake according to the recipe but for a few minutes longer.

cream cheese pastry

makes 10 pocket pies,
or 1 double-crusted 10-inch (25 cm) pie

For a novice baker, this is the most forgiving dough to work with. The cream cheese allows this pastry some elasticity but still produces tender and flaky results. It also adds a yummy crackery flavor to the crust.

8 tablespoons (1 stick/113 g) unsalted butter, at room temperature

4 ounces (113 g) cream cheese, at room temperature

¼ cup (60 mL) heavy cream

1½ cups plus 2 tablespoons (211 g) all-purpose flour, plus more for rolling out the dough

½ teaspoon coarse salt

Process the butter, cream cheese, and cream in a food processor or electric mixer or by hand to thoroughly combine.

Add the flour and salt. Process just until combined and the dough holds together in a ball. Turn the dough out onto a well-floured surface. Divide into 2 pieces. Flatten into disks and wrap each in plastic wrap.

Refrigerate for at least 30 minutes before rolling out. If the dough is chilled overnight, take it out 15 minutes before rolling out.

Rub flour all over a rolling pin. Working with one dough disk at a time, place the disk on a clean, well-floured surface. Applying some pressure with the rolling pin, roll gently from the center of the dough to the top and bottom edges. Rotate the disk and roll to the top and bottom edges again. Reflour the work surface and rolling pin, turn the dough over, and continue to roll the dough from the center out to the edges. Turn over and roll again, rotating the disk to ensure even rolling until the dough is about 12 inches (30 cm) in diameter and thin but not transparent.

spinach feta pocket pies

Substitute the chicken filling for spinach and feta for a vegetarian twist. This filling can also be doubled and made into a 10-inch (25 cm) round pie to serve in wedges.

To make the filling, heat 1 tablespoon extra-virgin olive oil in a medium skillet over medium heat. Add ½ cup (60 g) chopped onion and sauté until the onion is translucent, about 3 minutes. Stir in 2 cups (360 g) cooked spinach, squeezed of liquid and chopped (about 2 pounds, fresh) and ½ teaspoon coarse salt and cook to fully combine, about 2 minutes. Remove from the heat and cool slightly. Mix in 1 large egg, beaten, ¼ cup (38 g) crumbled feta cheese, and 2 tablespoons chopped fresh dill, or 1 tablespoon chopped dry dill. Chill. Form the pocket pies and bake as on page 51.

beef empanadas

makes 10 empanadas

Empanadas—pastry with a savory meat-and-vegetable filling—are a Spanish and South and Central American specialty and popular street food. Empanadas are usually fried, but these are a healthier baked version. You can make the filling up to 2 days in advance.

1 tablespoon olive oil

1 small onion, chopped

1 small green bell pepper, chopped

1 pound (454 g) ground beef

1 teaspoon ground cumin

¾ cup (108 g) pimiento-filled green olives, sliced

¾ cup (130 g) raisins

1 teaspoon honey

1 teaspoon coarse salt

¼ teaspoon freshly ground black pepper

Several dashes of hot sauce

2 large eggs, separated

1 recipe (2 disks) Cream Cheese Pastry (see page 52)

To make the filling, heat a large skillet over medium heat, and then swirl in the olive oil. Add the onion and bell pepper. Sauté until the onion is translucent, 3 to 4 minutes. Raise the heat to high and add the beef. Cook, stirring constantly, to brown, 5 to 7 minutes. Add the cumin and cook for another minute.

Stir in the olives, raisins, honey, salt, pepper, and hot sauce. Cook until the meat is golden brown, the liquid has evaporated, and the flavors have blended, about 4 more minutes. Cool the mixture to room temperature, then cool completely in the fridge. Stir in the egg whites.

Preheat the oven to 375°F (190°C) degrees. Butter or line a baking sheet.

To form the empanadas, work with half of a disk of dough at a time, rolling out on a floured surface. Using an overturned bowl (about 5 inches/13 cm across), cut out circles 3 or 4 at a time from each piece of dough. Gather all dough scraps together, reroll once, and cut. Place ¼ cup filling on one side of a dough circle. Wet the edges of the dough with water. Fold the dough over to form a half circle. Pinch the edges of the dough together. Crimp the edges with a fork. Repeat the process until all the filling is used. The empanadas can be frozen at this point (see page 51).

Place the empanadas on the prepared baking sheet and chill for a few minutes. Prick each pie on top twice with a fork. When ready to bake, beat the egg yolks with 1 tablespoon water. Brush the egg wash over each empanada. Bake for 20 to 25 minutes, until golden brown. Let rest for 5 minutes before serving. The empanadas can be cooled and frozen to reheat in a microwave.

MAKE THEM BITE-SIZE

For appetizers, follow the recipe but cut each piece of dough into 3-inch (8 cm) rounds. Fill with 1 to 2 teaspoons of filling. Bake for 12 to 15 minutes.

chicken chive burgers

makes 4 burgers

This burger is made from ground chicken that's spiked with chives, lemon juice, bread crumbs, and Dijon mustard to build a flavorful, juicy patty. For a completely healthy menu, add Baked Potato Poppers (page 20) in place of deep-fried French fries.

1½ pounds (680 g) ground chicken (light and dark meat)

1 teaspoon coarse salt

¼ teaspoon freshly ground black pepper

1 teaspoon Dijon mustard

⅓ cup (14 g) fresh bread crumbs

2 tablespoons fresh lemon juice

2 tablespoons chopped fresh chives

4 slices Fontina cheese (optional)

4 whole wheat hamburger buns

Optional garnishes: sliced tomato, sliced red onion, lettuce, mayo, Dijon mustard, and/or pickles

Preheat an outdoor grill or a grill pan to medium-high heat. Combine the chicken, salt, pepper, mustard, bread crumbs, lemon juice, and chives in a large bowl. Form into four ½-inch-thick (1 cm) patties.

Grill the patties, flipping once, until the juices run clear (the center should register 160°F/70°C on an instant-read thermometer), 8 to 10 minutes. Top the patties with the cheese (if using) during the last minute of cooking, and cover the grill or pan to melt it.

Meanwhile, lightly grill the cut side of the buns, if desired.

Serve with any or all of the garnishes.

burgers

makes 6 burgers

One thing is for sure: make a perfect burger, regardless of how you do it, and you make a happy man or woman. Though there are many roads to the perfect burger, ground meat and bun are mandatory basics—condiments and improvisation determine individual style (see page 61).

6 soft buns for hamburgers (see page 60)

1 tablespoon unsalted butter, softened

Coarse salt and freshly ground black pepper

2 pounds (1 kg) ground beef, formed into 6 patties

1 teaspoon Worcestershire sauce (optional)

6 slices mild cheddar cheese

½ red onion, thinly sliced (about ½ cup/106 g)

2 tablespoons mayonnaise

Ketchup (optional)

Mustard (optional)

3 lettuce leaves, cut in half

3 dill pickles, thinly cut horizontally

Preheat the broiler or preheat the oven to 400°F (200°C). Cut the buns in half and place them cut-side up on a rimmed baking sheet. Spread with the butter.

Heat a large skillet over high heat. Generously salt and pepper the beef patties. Space the patties in the skillet without touching and cook, without turning or flattening, for 4 to 6 minutes (depending on thickness). Turn the burgers and cook for another 4 to 6 minutes. If desired, swirl the Worcestershire into the pan 2 minutes before the burgers are finished. (Do this if you have inferior meat or no ketchup.)

With 1 minute left to cook, place a cheese slice on each burger. Cover with a pot lid and cook until melted. Lay onion slices on top of the melting cheese. (If using sautéed onions—see page 61— place under the cheese before melting.) Remove the burgers to a plate or board to rest for a few seconds before placing them on the buns.

Meanwhile, broil or toast the buns for 1 to 5 minutes, until golden on the cut side and still soft on the outside.

Spread mayonnaise on one side of each bun. Lay a burger on top. (Top with ketchup and mustard, if using.) Garnish with lettuce and top with the other half of the bun. Serve immediately with a side of sliced dill pickles.

BURGER TEMPLATE

GROUND BEEF

When choosing ground beef for a burger, fat content is important for flavor. If possible, be mindful of where your meat comes from—in the USA, you should check the USDA rating on your meat, beholden to standards of safety and quality. Wherever you live, it's wise to buy domestically produced meat. Most everyday supermarket shoppers will use supermarket ground chuck steak. Try combining a high-quality lean ground sirloin with a 75 percent lean ground chuck (higher in fat) for an upgraded flavor and texture. Buying it freshly ground from a butcher is even better. Aside from chuck, burger aficionados use a combination, which may include brisket, sirloin, flatiron, and skirt or hanger steak. Each cut of meat brings a different flavor and texture balance to the burger, just as different grape varietals combine to make a fine wine. Time permitting, bring the meat to room temperature for about 30 minutes before cooking to help it brown instead of steam. Consider the size of the patty (thin or thick, small or large), bun choice, and cooking method (broiled, grilled, or panfried). Form the patty slightly larger than the bun as it will shrink when cooked. For a tender and juicy result, handle the meat as little as possible. Salt and pepper each patty aggressively just before cooking.

BUNS

Consider the relationship of the bun to the meat. The bun must absorb the juices while holding together enough to accommodate both burger and topping. The way you choose to prepare the bun (plain or toasted? soft but heated?) affects the outcome, too. Here are some options.

- **Martin's potato roll**—Just firm enough to hold together but soft enough to marry well with the patty and condiments. Butter and toast to a light crisp on the inside, yet soft and warm on the outside.

- **English muffin**—Heresy to some but heaven to others who appreciate the firm platform and those crannies, which catch juice and sauce. The extra-large version is preferable for accommodating a large patty and a hungry person.

- **Brioche roll**—Buttery and soft.

- **Old-fashioned hamburger bun (soft)**—You have to toast, griddle, or heat for it to work well.

- **Kaiser-style roll (with or without seeds)**—Deli sandwich meets burger. Some find it too hard, but it makes for handy eating since it holds the add-ons well.

CONDIMENTS + ADD-ONS

- **Cheese**—Cheddar, Muenster, Monterey Jack, Colby, provolone, American, blue, or a combination thereof. Add sliced cheese, cover with a pot lid, and let melt with 1 minute left for the burger to cook (grated needs only 30 seconds).

- **Onions**—Red, white, yellow. If you want raw and slightly crunchy, a thinly sliced onion is best. If soft onions are preferred, sauté and deglaze first with vinegar or an alcohol such as bourbon, cognac, or wine.

- **Pickles, lettuce, tomato**—Sliced dill pickles add an acidic flavor balance; bread-and-butter pickles, a sweet one. Clean, dry lettuce leaves or shredded lettuce bring a fresh crunch. Thinly slice tomatoes with a serrated knife for their soft yet cool, moist texture. Pat dry if the slices are too wet.

- **Ketchup, American yellow or Dijon mustard, mayo**— Worcestershire or barbecue sauce can stand in for ketchup. If you're out of mayo, try butter.

- **Bacon**—Few people will refuse a bacon burger if it's offered.

COOKING METHOD

No matter the cooking method, if you want the burger to form a crust and retain its juicy moisture within, never move the burger until it has released from the pan's surface on its own.

- **Panfried**—Probably the most common home-cooking method. Get your skillet really hot before adding your burger. The relatively cool temperature of the meat and the coating of fat in the skillet will prevent burning. Turn only once, rather than "flipping" burgers. Be careful to scrape up every brown bit. (Open a window or turn on a fan.)

- **Grilled**—Start with a hot grill. Coals must be gray and very hot, otherwise the meat will steam and absorb smoke flavor before forming a crust.

- **Broiler**—Flame-broiled is heralded by many a burger joint, but at home there is rarely enough flame. Broiling is less odorous than stovetop panfrying and thus is favored by some, but rarely are the results as good as panfrying. Turn on the broiler, then heat the broiling pan for several minutes before adding the meat for best results.

italian pressed sandwiches

serves 6

This pressed sandwich borrows the flavors of a classic hero, but with less bread, more filling, and a compact result. Lay out sandwich fixings—your choice—on a whole loaf of bread that's been halved lengthwise, then cut it into several sections for a quick and efficient way to make multiple sandwiches.

1 rectangular ciabatta or other thick-crusted bread, about 18 by 5 inches (46 by 13 cm)

1½ tablespoons extra-virgin olive oil

4 ounces (¼ pound/113 g) prosciutto, thinly sliced

4 ounces (¼ pound/113 g) hard salami, thinly sliced

8 ounces (½ pound/227 g) fresh mozzarella cheese, sliced

Freshly ground black pepper

⅛ teaspoon dried oregano

5 whole sun-dried tomatoes in oil, thinly sliced

Slice the bread horizontally and lay each half, cut-side up, on a work surface. Drizzle with the olive oil. On one half, lay down the prosciutto to cover. Repeat with the salami and mozzarella. Top with the pepper, oregano, and sun-dried tomatoes. Cover with the other half of the bread.

Press down on the sandwich and wrap tightly in plastic wrap and then foil. Press under heavy saucepans or cans for up to overnight in the refrigerator. When ready to eat or pack, unwrap the loaf, cut into servings, and serve or rewrap and pack.

classic french dip

makes 6 sandwiches, with leftover meat

This French dip sandwich is actually three recipes in one: a braised boneless chuck roast, a jus made from the braising liquid, and the assembled sandwich. The sandwich is crunchy on the outside, soft, melty, and unctuous on the inside. The bread stays crisp but then instantly softens when dipped in the jus—impossible for any meat lover to resist.

2 tablespoons extra-virgin olive oil, plus more for drizzling

1 (3-pound/1.3 kg) boneless chuck roast

1 tablespoon coarse salt

½ teaspoon freshly ground black pepper

1 large yellow onion, chopped

2 medium carrots, peeled and chopped

2 celery stalks, chopped

4 garlic cloves, minced

2 tablespoons tomato paste

1 cup (240 mL) dry red wine

3 cups (720 mL) chicken or beef broth

2 bay leaves

1 baguette

4 ounces (113 g) sliced Swiss cheese

Preheat the oven to 350°F (180°C) with a rack in the lower-third position. Heat a Dutch oven over medium-high heat. Add the oil. Season the meat with the salt and pepper. When the oil shimmers, add the meat to the pot and brown on both sides, about 8 minutes total. Transfer to a plate.

Add the onions, carrots, celery, and garlic to the pot and sauté until soft and golden, about 10 minutes. Stir in the tomato paste and cook for 1 minute. Add the wine and bring to a boil, scraping up the brown bits from the bottom of the pot. Boil to reduce the liquid by half.

Return the chuck roast to the Dutch oven, add 2 cups (480 mL) of the chicken or beef broth and the bay leaves, and bring to a boil. Cover, transfer to the oven, and cook, basting a few times, until the meat is falling-apart tender, about 3 hours.

Transfer the meat to a baking dish and shred using two forks. Strain the liquid through a fine-mesh sieve into a small saucepan, pressing on the solids to extract as much liquid as possible. Add the remaining 1 cup (240 mL) broth and keep jus warm on the stovetop until ready to serve.

Preheat the broiler. Slice the baguette lengthwise in half, drizzle with oil, and place on a baking sheet. Mound with the shredded meat to cover the bread, top with the Swiss cheese, and broil until the cheese is bubbly, about 2 minutes.

Cut the sandwich into 6 portions and serve immediately, with a bowl of jus on the side.

tuna salad sandwich

makes 4 to 6 sandwiches

To get the right ratio of tuna to scallions, put the tuna in the mixing bowl first and slowly add the scallion; too much scallion is off-putting, but you need just enough to boost and complement the tuna flavor. Take the same care with the mayonnaise, too, by slowly mixing it in at the end.

2 (6-ounce/170 g) cans water-packed white tuna

1 large scallion (both white and green parts), finely chopped, or ¼ cup (30 g) chopped or grated onion

1 celery stalk, chopped

1 tablespoon fresh lemon juice (from ½ lemon)

¼ teaspoon freshly ground black pepper

¼ teaspoon coarse salt, plus more to taste

¼ cup (54 g) mayonnaise, or to taste

8 to 12 slices whole-grain or rye bread

8 to 12 lettuce leaves, washed and patted dry

1 to 3 dashes of Tabasco sauce (optional)

2 pickles of choice, finely chopped (optional)

1 teaspoon capers, rinsed (optional)

¼ teaspoon chopped fresh dill (optional)

Drain the tuna and place it in a bowl. Break up the chunks with a fork. Add the scallion and toss together. Mix in the celery, lemon juice, pepper, and salt and any optional add-ins.

Little by little, mix in the mayonnaise until the desired consistency is reached. Spread the tuna salad on plain or toasted bread, topped with lettuce.

NOTE

For tuna melts, omit the lettuce. Toast 8 to 12 slices of bread. Top the toast with tuna salad and top with 1 slice of cheddar, Swiss, or white American cheese. Broil in a toaster oven or broiler for 3 minutes, or until the cheese is melted.

jerk chicken and mango chutney sandwiches

makes 12 sandwiches

In this grab-and-go sandwich, homemade jerk sauce flavors a chicken cutlet while tangy-sweet mango chutney offsets the spicy meat. Try spreading a little coconut oil on each roll—it's not necessary, but it's so, so good and adds to the tropical flavor of the sandwich. Serve these at a party with ice-cold beer.

5 bunches scallions, trimmed and roughly chopped

3 large garlic cloves, peeled

3 Scotch bonnet chiles (seeded, if concerned about the heat)

2 sprigs fresh thyme, leaves removed, or 2 teaspoons dried

¼ cup (32 g) ground allspice

2 tablespoons freshly ground black pepper

1½ tablespoons coarse salt

½ cup (120 mL) water

4 pounds (1.8 kg) skinless, boneless chicken thighs, trimmed (and halved if pieces are too large to fit on bun)

12 soft hamburger rolls, such as Martin's potato rolls

¼ cup (60 mL) coconut oil (optional)

¾ cup (228 g) mango chutney, homemade (recipe follows) or store-bought

Working in two batches, in the bowl of a food processor, combine the scallions, garlic, chiles, thyme leaves, allspice, pepper, and salt; pulse a few times for a rough texture. With the processor running, add ¼ cup (60 mL) of the water per batch through the feed tube to make a coarse sauce. Set aside ½ cup (120 mL) for serving. (Alternatively, the scallions, garlic, and chiles can be minced with a knife and combined with the remaining ingredients.)

Place the chicken in a large bowl, baking dish, or resealable plastic bag. Pierce the chicken with a fork. Pour the sauce over the chicken, turning to coat. Cover and refrigerate, turning occasionally, for at least 2 hours and up to 24 hours.

continued

Prepare a grill, or place a grill pan over high heat. Place the chicken on a relatively cool part of the grill. If using a grill pan, reduce the heat to medium. Cook for 15 minutes, brushing the chicken with the marinade a couple of times. Flip the chicken over and repeat the process until slightly charred and an instant-read thermometer reads 160°F (70°C), about 15 minutes more. (Alternatively, preheat the oven to 425°F/220°C and bake for 40 minutes, turning once halfway through.) Remove from the heat and let rest for 10 minutes.

Spread some coconut oil on the inside of each roll, if using. Put a piece of chicken on the bottom part of each roll and spread a tablespoon of chutney and the reserved sauce, as desired, on each before closing the roll and serving.

mango chutney

makes 3 cups (912 g)

4 mangoes, peeled, pitted, and chopped (about 4 cups/660 g)

3 tablespoons grated fresh ginger

1 medium onion, chopped (about 2 cups/240 g)

1 garlic clove, minced

½ red bell pepper, chopped

⅓ cup (66 g) sugar

2 teaspoons salt

½ cup (120 mL) white vinegar

⅓ cup (80 mL) water

½ cup (85 g) raisins (optional)

Mix all the ingredients in a medium nonreactive pot. Bring to a boil over high heat, then reduce the heat to low and simmer, stirring occasionally, for 1 hour and 15 minutes. Remove the chutney from the heat and let cool. Store in the refrigerator for up to 2 months.

banh mi

serves 4 to 6

The banh mi sandwich is a quintessential representation of the French colonial presence in Indochina (Vietnam), where the French left their taste for baguettes and pâté and the Vietnamese added fresh vegetables, herbs, and lightly pickled veggies. This homemade version is a refreshing twist on the sandwich, one of the most universally loved lunchtime fares.

MARINADE

¼ cup plus 1 tablespoon (75 mL) dark soy sauce

2 tablespoons fish sauce

1 (2-inch/5 cm) piece of ginger, peeled and minced

3 garlic cloves, minced

1 large shallot, minced

2 tablespoons finely chopped palm sugar or brown sugar

2 tablespoons safflower oil

½ teaspoon freshly ground black pepper

12 ounces (¾ pound/340 g) pork tenderloin, cut crosswise into 1-inch-wide (3 cm) pieces

PICKLED VEGETABLES

¾ cup (180 mL) white vinegar

½ cup (120 mL) water

2 tablespoons granulated sugar

1 teaspoon coarse salt

1 cup (73 g) julienned carrots

1 cup (73 g) julienned daikon

1 baguette

⅓ cup (72 g) mayonnaise

1 teaspoon chili paste, such as sambal oelek

6 ounces (170 g) store-bought pork pâté, thinly sliced

4 ounces (113 g) thinly sliced ham, such as Black Forest (sliced by the deli)

⅓ English cucumber, cut into 8 spears

8 cilantro sprigs

1 jalapeño, thinly sliced

continued

Combine all the marinade ingredients in a medium bowl.

Add the pork tenderloin, stir to coat evenly, and let marinate for 30 minutes.

To make the pickled vegetables, bring the vinegar, water, sugar, and salt to a boil in a small saucepan, stirring to dissolve the sugar. Add the carrots and daikon, remove from the heat, and let cool to room temperature.

Preheat a grill pan over high heat. Grill the pork, turning once, until an instant-read thermometer inserted into the center registers 140°F (60°C), about 4 minutes total. Remove the pork from the grill pan, let rest for 5 minutes, and thinly slice.

Preheat the broiler with the rack in the upper-third position. Halve the baguette lengthwise. Place cut-side up directly on the oven rack and broil until toasted and brown around the edges, 2 minutes. Remove from the oven.

Combine the mayonnaise and chili paste in a small bowl, then spread evenly across the bottom of the baguette. Top with the pâté, ham, and grilled pork. Distribute the cucumber spears, pickled vegetables, cilantro sprigs, and jalapeños evenly over the meats. Close the baguette, cut into portions, and serve.

PRODUCTION-LINE SANDWICH MAKING

When making banh mi or Italian pressed sandwiches (see page 63) for a group, I start with one large loaf, split it horizontally, layer in the filling, wrap in plastic wrap, and refrigerate. It's a clever do-in-advance technique. Leaving it whole means it stays fresher longer and allows the flavors to meld—just slice into single portions when ready.

beef satay with thai peanut sauce

makes 20 skewers

This marinated meat is threaded on skewers and grilled, but it's the creamy peanut sauce that really grabs one's attention. These skewers will be a smash hit at your table. Thinly sliced boneless chicken can be substituted for the beef.

¼ cup (60 mL) peanut oil

1 large shallot, minced

2 garlic cloves, minced

1 (2-inch/5 cm) piece ginger, peeled and minced

¼ cup (60 mL) low-sodium soy sauce

1 teaspoon turmeric

1 teaspoon ground coriander

¼ cup (60 mL) fresh lime juice

¼ teaspoon freshly ground black pepper

1 pound (454 g) flank steak, sliced ⅛ inch (3 mm) thick against the grain

Thai Peanut Sauce (recipe follows)

About 20 wooden skewers

> ### NOTE
>
> Wooden skewers must always be soaked in water before using on a grill. Otherwise, the wood will burn before the meat is cooked.

Whisk together the peanut oil, shallot, garlic, ginger, soy sauce, turmeric, coriander, lime juice, and pepper in an 8-inch square baking dish or wide shallow bowl. Add the beef, tossing to combine, and marinate up to 1 hour at room temperature, or up to 4 hours in the fridge.

Meanwhile, soak the skewers in water for 30 minutes (see Note); drain.

Preheat an outdoor grill or a grill pan over medium-high heat. Thread 1 slice of beef onto each skewer. Grill the beef, turning once, just until cooked through, about 2 minutes total. Serve with the peanut sauce.

thai peanut sauce

makes about 3 cups (720 ml)

1 cup plus 1 tablespoon (159 g) unsalted roasted peanuts

1 garlic clove, smashed and peeled

2 tablespoons finely chopped palm sugar or light brown sugar

2 tablespoons fish sauce

1 tablespoon low-sodium soy sauce

1 ½ cups (360 mL) unsweetened coconut milk

1 teaspoon Asian sesame oil

1 tablespoon fresh lime juice

¼ cup (21 g) unsweetened shredded coconut

Combine 1 cup (150 g) of the peanuts with the remaining ingredients in a blender and blend until smooth. Transfer to a serving bowl.

Chop the remaining tablespoon of peanuts and sprinkle over the sauce before serving.

new york city hot dog

makes 6 dogs

Like the ubiquitous street-cart New York City hot dog, this one is served on a steamed bun with a red-tinged onion relish and sauerkraut.

RELISH

2 tablespoons extra-virgin olive oil
1 medium yellow onion, finely chopped
¼ teaspoon coarse salt
1 garlic clove, minced
1 tablespoon tomato paste
½ cup (120 mL) water
2 tablespoons red wine vinegar
½ teaspoon hot sauce
1 teaspoon sugar

6 all-beef hot dogs
6 hot dog buns
Spicy brown mustard
Quick Kraut (recipe follows)

For the relish, heat a small saucepan over medium-high heat. Add the oil. When it shimmers, add the onions and salt and cook, stirring occasionally, until the onions are soft and golden brown in places, 8 to 10 minutes.

Add the garlic and cook for 1 minute, until fragrant. Stir in the tomato paste, water, red wine vinegar, hot sauce, and sugar and bring to a boil, then simmer a couple of minutes. Remove from the heat.

Bring 1 inch (2 cm) of water to a boil in a deep skillet. Add the hot dogs, reduce the heat, keeping the water at a bare simmer, and heat through, at least 8 minutes (or until ready to serve).

Place a steamer basket in a pot over boiling water. Add the hot dog buns, cover, and steam the buns for 2 minutes to warm them. (Or put the buns on a plate and microwave them for 1 minute.)

Put the hot dogs in the buns and let guests dress their own dogs, or top each with some onion relish, spicy brown mustard, and sauerkraut and serve immediately.

quick kraut

makes 3 cups (720 g)

2 tablespoons extra-virgin olive oil

1 small yellow onion, halved lengthwise and thinly sliced crosswise

½ teaspoon coarse salt

½ head green cabbage, cored and thinly sliced

½ cup (120 mL) apple cider vinegar

½ cup (120 mL) water

⅓ cup (80 mL) apple cider or apple juice

Heat a medium saucepan over medium-high heat. Add the oil. When it shimmers, add the onions and salt and cook, stirring occasionally, until the onions are soft and translucent, 3 minutes. Add the cabbage, vinegar, water, and apple cider, and stir to combine. Bring to a boil, cover, reduce the heat, and simmer until the cabbage is tender, 30 to 35 minutes.

Let cool if not using immediately. Transfer to a container with a tight-fitting lid. The kraut can be stored in the refrigerator for up to 1 month.

double-decker pork tacos

makes 1 taco

These aren't your average tacos: two tortillas layered with melted cheese are stuffed with various fillings that make for a deluxe experience. Feel free to swap out the pork for something else you have on hand—the fillings from Pepper Steak Fajitas (page 81) or Spicy Shrimp Tacos (page 80) work well.

2 teaspoons vegetable oil or lard

¼ cup (45 g) cooked chorizo, cubed

¼ white onion, chopped

2 corn tortillas

1 slice mild, melting cheese, such as Monterey Jack, or Mexican melting cheese, such as queso asadero

1 tablespoon Basic Salsa (page 13) or store-bought

Heat a large (preferably cast-iron) skillet over high heat. Swirl in 1 teaspoon of the oil and sauté the chorizo and onions until the onions are soft and golden. Transfer the chorizo and onions to a plate and wipe the skillet clean.

Add the remaining 1 teaspoon oil and place the tortillas in the pan. When the bottoms are toasted, about 1 minute, flip them both over.

Place the cheese on a tortilla. Take the other tortilla and place the toasted side against the cheese. Cook until the cheese has completely melted. Add the chorizo and salsa, fold over, and serve.

spicy shrimp tacos

serves 4 to 6

Plump shrimp are tossed with a fresh combination of spicy green chiles, herbaceous cilantro, and tangy lime juice, folded into warm corn tortillas, to deliver big, assertive flavors that satisfy that south-of-the-border hankering. This recipe uses both oil and butter to sauté the shrimp because the oil withstands the high heat while the butter brings flavor.

1 pound (454 g) medium-large shrimp, peeled

Coarse salt and ground red pepper, such as cayenne, or black pepper

1 tablespoon extra-virgin olive oil

1 tablespoon unsalted butter

1 large fresh green chile, such as serrano or jalapeño

6 garlic cloves, minced

Juice of 1 lime

1½ cups (96 g) minced fresh cilantro leaves

12 corn tortillas, toasted and stacked in a towel to steam

3 tomatoes, cored and chopped

½ head romaine lettuce, shredded

1 lime, cut into 12 wedges, for serving

Pat the shrimp dry with a towel and season all over with salt and pepper. Heat a large skillet over medium-high heat. Swirl in the oil. When it shimmers, add the butter and let it melt. Add the shrimp in a single layer and cook, without moving, for 2 minutes. Flip the shrimp and add the chile and garlic. Stir continuously for 2 minutes more, regulating the heat to avoid burning the garlic.

Turn off the heat and stir in the lime juice and cilantro. Place a few shrimp in each tortilla, add some tomato and lettuce, and serve with lime wedges.

pepper steak fajitas

serves 4 to 6

This beloved Tex-Mex dish is easy to make at home with sliced beef, a few vegetables, and a stack of tortillas. Top round steak is typical for fajitas, but flank, skirt, or hanger steak, thinly sliced across the grain, works equally well.

4 garlic cloves, minced

Juice of 2 limes

1½ pounds (680 g) top round steaks, pounded and scored with a knife tip in a crosshatch pattern, or skirt steak

Coarse salt and freshly ground black pepper

1 tablespoon vegetable oil

1 red or green bell pepper, cored, seeded, and sliced

1 onion, sliced

12 flour or corn tortillas, warmed

Combine the garlic and lime juice in a small bowl and set aside. Heat a large heavy skillet (preferably cast-iron) over high heat. Generously season the meat on both sides with salt and black pepper.

Swirl half the oil in the hot skillet. When it shimmers, add the meat and sear for 2 minutes on each side for medium-rare. Transfer the steaks to a plate (leaving the skillet on the heat) and pour the garlic-lime mixture over them.

Reduce the heat to medium-high and swirl the remaining oil in the skillet. Add the bell peppers and onions and sauté until soft and golden brown around the edges, 8 to 10 minutes.

Slice the steak and return it to the skillet along with any accumulated juices. Serve the fajitas in the skillet with the tortillas on the side.

quick fried chicken

serves 4

Fried chicken on the table in 45 minutes? Here it is, the quick recipe. Serve with Loaded Potato Skins (page 28), Mac 'n' Cheese (page 88), and Cheddar Corn Bread (page 96) for a taste of a Southern-style feast.

4 cups (1 L) buttermilk or milk

2 tablespoons Tabasco or other hot sauce

1 (3- to 3½-pound/1.3 to 1.5 kg) chicken, cut into 8 pieces (see Note) and each breast cut in half again (reserve the neck, back, and wing tips for another purpose)

1 cup (130 g) all-purpose flour

1½ teaspoons coarse salt, plus a little more for sprinkling

½ teaspoon freshly ground black pepper

¼ teaspoon cayenne pepper

2 cups (480 mL) peanut oil, vegetable oil, bacon fat, or lard

In a 9 by 13-inch (23 by 33 cm) baking dish, stir together the buttermilk and Tabasco. Submerge the chicken parts in the mixture and leave as long as possible, at least 10 minutes (but up to overnight—in the fridge—is even better).

In a plastic or paper bag, combine the flour, salt, black pepper, and cayenne.

Shake the chicken parts, 2 or 3 pieces at a time, in the flour. Repeat with the remaining chicken. Shake off the excess flour. In a 14-inch (36 cm) skillet (or two smaller skillets), heat 2 inches of oil over high heat until very hot. Test with a tiny bit of chicken skin. If the oil bubbles immediately, it is hot enough.

Place the chicken in the hot oil. Evenly distribute as many pieces as will fit in one layer in the pan, leaving ½ inch (1 cm) between pieces, and leave to fry undisturbed for about 15 minutes. Lower the heat as necessary to prevent excessive browning before the meat is cooked properly; the oil should continue to bubble steadily.

Turn the pieces and cook for an additional 15 to 20 minutes.

Remove to a rack to drain. Repeat the process to cook all the chicken.

To keep the first batch warm, place on a rimmed baking sheet in a 200°F (90°C) oven. Sprinkle with salt and serve.

NOTE

Cutting apart a whole bird is a matter of finding that sweet spot in the joint through which to cut with a sharp knife. A good pair of kitchen shears makes quick work of cutting up both sides of the backbone and through the breastbone.

A bird can easily be cut into eight standard pieces—save the backbones, neck, bones, and wing tips in the freezer, and when you have enough, make chicken broth.

richie's grilled baby back ribs

serves 4

Ribs are a most beloved meal, and it seems like you can never make enough when the whole crew is together. This recipe is cooked on a grill, but if you're cooking the ribs in the oven (see sidebar, opposite), you'll need to add more seasoning to assure an authentic taste; to approximate the deep flavor of barbecue smoke, add one tablespoon each of cocoa and instant coffee to the rub.

2 racks (4 pounds/1.8 kg total) baby back ribs or pork spareribs

Coarse salt and freshly ground black pepper

2 teaspoons sweet paprika

½ teaspoon smoked Spanish paprika (if available)

1 teaspoon dried sage

½ teaspoon ground cinnamon

½ teaspoon ground cumin

¼ teaspoon cayenne pepper

2 tablespoons granulated brown sugar

1 cup (240 mL) favorite barbecue sauce

Sprinkle the ribs generously with salt and black pepper. In a small bowl, combine the sweet and smoked paprikas, sage, cinnamon, cumin, cayenne, and brown sugar. Rub the mixture into the meat and let stand at room temperature for at least 30 minutes or refrigerated for up to 2 hours.

Prepare a charcoal grill for indirect heat. (If oven-roasting, see sidebar, opposite.)

Place the ribs on the grill, on very low heat, 250°F (120°C) or less. Remember, don't cook ribs over direct flames. Cover and almost close the vents. Every 20 minutes, turn the ribs around to cook evenly. They should be perfectly cooked within 1 ½ to 2 hours; if using pork spareribs, cook an additional half an hour. Serve with barbecue sauce on the side.

OVEN-ROASTING AS AN ALTERNATIVE

Place rub-seasoned ribs on a baking sheet and cook for 1½ to 2 hours at 350°F (180°C). Increase the heat to 425°F (220°C), brush over barbecue sauce, and cook for 15 more minutes until caramelized.

sicilian-style deep-dish pizza

serves 4 to 6

This is a thick, doughy, focaccia-like crust baked with slow-roasted tomatoes and a conservative amount of sharp cheese—rather than laden with mozzarella. The tomatoes can be made in advance, as can the dough, which needs to rise overnight in the refrigerator.

1⅓ cups (315 mL) water

1 teaspoon sugar

1¼-ounce package (2¼ teaspoons/7 g) active dry yeast

3 cups plus 1 tablespoon (398 g) all-purpose flour

¼ cup (35 g) cornmeal

1 teaspoon coarse salt

¼ cup (60 mL) olive oil, plus more for the bowl

Slow-Roasted Tomatoes (recipe follows)

¼ cup (30 g) grated Parmesan or Pecorino Romano cheese

Combine the water, sugar, and yeast in a medium bowl and let stand for 3 to 4 minutes to dissolve the yeast.

Whisk together 3 cups (390 g) of the flour, the cornmeal, and salt in another medium bowl. Slowly add one-third of the flour mixture to the yeast mixture, stirring with a wooden spoon; then add another third and stir. Add the olive oil, then the remaining flour, and stir.

Sprinkle the remaining tablespoon of flour on a countertop, turn out the dough, and knead until smooth. Transfer the dough to a large oiled bowl and turn to coat in oil. Cover and let rise overnight in the refrigerator.

The next day, oil a rimmed baking sheet. On a lightly floured board, roll the dough out to the size of the pan. Fit the dough into the pan and let rest for 30 minutes.

Preheat the oven to 450°F (230°C) with a rack in the center position. Spread the tomatoes evenly over the dough. Bake for about 30 minutes, until the tomatoes are bubbling and the dough is golden brown. Remove from the oven and sprinkle on the grated cheese.

slow-roasted tomatoes

makes 4 to 6 cups (960 g to 1.4 kg)

These can be made up to 2 days ahead.

12 medium tomatoes, sliced ¼ inch
(6 mm) thick

4 shallots, thinly sliced

10–12 thyme sprigs

½ cup (120 mL) olive oil

1 teaspoon coarse salt

Preheat the oven to 300°F
(150°C) with a rack in the center
position. Arrange the tomatoes in
a single layer on 2 baking sheets.
Scatter the shallots and thyme
sprigs over the tomatoes, drizzle
with the olive oil, and sprinkle
with the salt.

Roast for 2 to 2½ hours, turning
the tomatoes a few times, until
wilted and browning in places.
Let cool. Store in a sealed
container in the refrigerator.

mac 'n' cheese

serves 6

A tray of this crunchy-topped, gooey goodness—assembled and baked in under an hour—is the perfect partner for Quick Fried Chicken (page 82).

1 pound (454 g) elbow macaroni (or any pasta shape)

4 tablespoons (57 g) unsalted butter

¼ cup (33 g) all-purpose flour

4 cups (1 quart/1 L) whole milk

2¾ cups (12 ounces/340 g) shredded cheese (cheddar, Muenster, Monterey Jack—whatever you have in the fridge)

¼ teaspoon freshly ground black pepper

Pinch of cayenne pepper

1½ cups (120 g) panko bread crumbs, or homemade (see Note)

2 tablespoons unsalted butter, melted

Hot sauce, such as Frank's Hot Red Sauce, for serving

Preheat the oven to 375°F (190°C) with a rack in the center position. Butter a 2½- to 3-quart (2.5 to 3 L) baking dish.

Cook the pasta in a large pot of boiling salted water until al dente. Drain and return to the pot.

While the pasta cooks, melt the 4 tablespoons (57 g) butter in a large saucepan over medium-high heat. Whisk in the flour and cook, whisking constantly, until the roux is golden and fragrant, about 2 minutes. Whisk in the milk, bring to a boil, and boil, whisking constantly, until thickened, about 5 minutes. Remove from the heat and add the cheese gradually, stirring until smooth; add the black pepper and cayenne with the last of the cheese. Pour the cheese sauce over the pasta and stir to combine. Transfer to the prepared baking dish.

To make the topping, combine the panko with the melted butter in a small bowl. Sprinkle over the macaroni and cheese and bake for 18 to 20 minutes, until golden on top.

Serve with the hot sauce.

Let some bread dry out overnight. Preheat the oven to 250°F (120°C) and tear the bread into little bits. Dry the crumbs in the oven for 10 minutes. Blend in a food processor or blender, working in batches if necessary, to the desired consistency. (If you don't have time for air-drying, dry in a 250°F/120°C oven for 30 minutes.)

chili

serves 6

Whether it's the Super Bowl, game night, or just a plain Tuesday dinner, this chili can be dressed up and down for any occasion. Always serve it with some combination of fixings, such as grated cheese, sour cream, sliced avocados, chopped tomatoes, chopped onion or scallions, or minced cilantro. Make the Cheddar Corn Bread (page 96) to serve alongside.

5 dried red chiles (Mexican ancho, New Mexican Hatch, or Anaheim; see Note)

1 tablespoon olive oil

1 cup (120 g) chopped onion

3 garlic cloves, minced (1 tablespoon)

2 pounds (1 kg) ground beef

1 tablespoon coarse salt

1 teaspoon ground cumin

¼ teaspoon crushed red pepper flakes, or pinch of cayenne pepper

½ teaspoon dried oregano

1 bay leaf

¼ cup (28 g) pickled jalapeños, chopped (optional)

1 (28-ounce/794 g) can tomatoes, broken up, with juice

1½ cups (12 ounces/360 mL) beer

1 (15-ounce/425 g) can beans (pinto, kidney, black, or a combination), drained

In a dry large skillet over high heat, lightly toast both sides of the chiles for a few minutes. After roasting, remove from pan to slice open, then remove and discard the stem and seeds. Cover the chiles in boiling water and let soften for 5 minutes. In a blender or food processor, puree the chiles with enough soaking liquid to form a thick paste.

Heat the skillet again over medium-high heat, and then add the olive oil. Sauté the onion and garlic until translucent, about 3 minutes. Increase the heat and add the beef and 2 teaspoons of the salt. Brown the beef, about 15 minutes. If the meat is excessively fatty (your judgment call), spoon off some of the fat, but leave some for flavor.

continued

Stir in the cumin and cook for 30 seconds. Add the chile paste, red pepper flakes, oregano, bay leaf, jalapeños, and the remaining teaspoon of salt. Stir to combine well.

Add the tomatoes and beer and simmer for 30 minutes. Add the beans and cook for an additional 20 minutes. Add water if needed for desired consistency. Serve with preferred condiments (see headnote).

NOTE

If you dry a fresh green poblano chile, you wind up with a red Mexican ancho chile. Its flavor—earthy and mildly spicy yet slightly fruity—lends a marvelous depth to chili, sauces, and stews. New Mexican Hatch or dried red Anaheim chiles can also be used in place of ancho.

pulled pork

serves 6 to 8 as a main dish or makes enough for 8 to 10 sandwiches

Pork shoulder gives you excellent bang for your buck, since it flavorfully feeds a large crowd at a very affordable price. Just plan ahead for its 3- to 4-hour cooking time. Serve on its own or with all the fixings. Either way, slather it with the tangy vinegar-based North Carolina–style barbecue sauce, which is thinner than most tomato-based barbecue sauces.

⅓ cup (75 g) packed light brown sugar

1 tablespoon ground cumin

1 teaspoon paprika

1 tablespoon coarse salt

½ teaspoon freshly ground black pepper

1 (6-pound/2.7 kg) boneless pork shoulder roast

3 cups (24 ounces/720 mL) Guinness

6 garlic cloves, smashed and peeled

North Carolina BBQ Sauce (recipe follows)

For the pork, preheat the oven to 350°F (180°C) with a rack in the lower-third position. Combine the brown sugar, cumin, paprika, salt, and pepper in a small bowl.

Rub the spice mixture all over the pork. Put the pork fat-side up in a 5- to 6-quart (5 to 5.5 L) Dutch oven. Pour the Guinness over the meat. Add the garlic cloves and bring to a boil over high heat.

Cover the pot, transfer to the oven, and braise, basting a few times, for 3 to 4 hours, until the pork is fork-tender. Remove from the oven and shred the pork with two forks. Stir to incorporate with the braising liquid.

Serve with the barbecue sauce.

north carolina bbq sauce

makes 1 cup (240 ml)

This sauce can be made up to 2 weeks ahead. Cool to room temperature,
transfer to a container with a tight-fitting lid, and store in the refrigerator.

8 tablespoons (1 stick/113 g) unsalted butter

1 tablespoon tomato paste

2 tablespoons light brown sugar

1 teaspoon coarse salt

¼ teaspoon freshly ground black pepper

1 teaspoon cayenne pepper

½ cup (120 mL) apple cider vinegar

2 tablespoons fresh lemon juice

1 teaspoon hot sauce, such as Tabasco

Melt the butter in a medium saucepan over medium heat. Add the tomato paste, brown sugar, salt, pepper, cayenne, and vinegar, raise the heat, and boil, whisking constantly, until the sugar and salt dissolve, about 1 minute. Remove from the heat and whisk in the lemon juice and hot sauce. Let cool to room temperature before serving.

cheddar corn bread

serves 6 to 8

This corn bread pairs great with Chili (page 90) or even ribs (see page 84). The addition of whole corn kernels makes the texture a little more interesting, but you can leave them out with no problem. Ditto the pickled jalapeños. If you don't have a 10-inch (25 cm) cast-iron skillet, use an 8-inch (20 cm) square baking pan and adjust the baking time.

1 cup (130 g) all-purpose flour

1 cup (140 g) stone-ground yellow cornmeal

1 tablespoon sugar

1½ teaspoons baking powder

1 teaspoon coarse salt

Pinch of cayenne pepper

1½ cups (360 mL) milk

2 large eggs, lightly beaten

1½ tablespoons unsalted butter, melted

1 cup (120 g) grated cheddar cheese

½ cup (83 g) corn kernels (frozen, fresh, or left over from a cooked cob)

2 tablespoons chopped pickled jalapeños (optional)

Preheat the oven to 425°F (220°C).

In a large bowl, whisk together the flour, cornmeal, sugar, baking powder, salt, and cayenne. Blend in the milk, eggs, and butter. Fold in the cheese, corn, and the jalapeños, if using.

Place in a well-seasoned 10-inch (25 cm) cast-iron skillet or a buttered 8-inch (20 cm) square baking pan and smooth over the top. Bake for 35 to 45 minutes, until the top is golden brown and a cake tester inserted in the center comes out clean. Do not overbake or the corn bread will be dry. Cut into wedges or squares and serve hot.

DRINKS

spiked (or not) tarragon lemonade

serves 6

Simple syrup is an awesome way to customize your own cocktail flavors. The syrup, usually equal parts sugar and water heated until the sugar dissolves, readily absorbs the flavor of any ingredient steeped in it. There's something special about the combo of lemon and tarragon here. Without any alcohol, it's a great "soft" cocktail to serve; gin makes it "hard."

1 cup (200 g) sugar

4 cups (1 L) water

Leaves from 6 tarragon sprigs, plus 6 sprigs for garnish

2 cups (480 mL) fresh lemon juice (from 10 to 12 lemons)

1½ cups (12 ounces/360 mL) gin (optional)

Combine the sugar and 1 cup (240 mL) of the water in a small saucepan and add the tarragon leaves, rubbing them between your palms. Bring to a boil, stirring until the sugar is dissolved. Let cool to room temperature. Strain out the tarragon.

Combine the lemon juice, tarragon simple syrup, and the remaining 3 cups (720 mL) cold water in a large pitcher. Refrigerate until ready to serve.

To serve, fill 6 glasses with ice. If using the gin, pour a shot over the ice in each glass. Add the lemonade and garnish each with a tarragon sprig.

black tea and citrus pitcher

serves 6 to 8

Your morning tea and orange juice combined into one game day–worthy beverage. It's a refreshing drink to serve at a barbecue with smoky-flavored grilled foods, such as Richie's Grilled Baby Back Ribs (page 84).

3 bags black tea or 1 tablespoon loose tea leaves

4 cups (1 L) boiling water

2 tablespoons sugar

1 lemon, halved lengthwise and thinly sliced crosswise

2 cups (480 mL) fresh orange juice

Put the tea bags (or tea) in a large heatproof pitcher, add the boiling water, and let steep for 5 minutes.

Remove the tea bags (or strain out the tea) and add the sugar, stirring to dissolve. Stir in the lemon slices and orange juice and refrigerate until cold.

To serve, pour into tall glasses filled with ice.

thrice-spiced bloody mary

serves 6

There is no need to buy flavor-spiked tomato juice when you can infuse the juice yourself at home with, for example, an onion, a garlic clove, or a chili. If you're a Bloody Mary drinker, this will become your new favorite recipe.

1 (46-ounce/1.36 L) can tomato juice

1 onion, halved

1 clove garlic, smashed and peeled

1 jalapeño

1¼ to 1½ cups (10 to 12 ounces/300 to 360 mL) pepper vodka, or plain

1 tablespoon Worcestershire sauce

½ teaspoon Tabasco or other hot sauce

¼ teaspoon freshly ground black pepper

1½ tablespoons prepared horseradish

Juice of 1 lemon

Garnishes: pickled okra, sliced cucumber, thinly sliced radishes, and/or celery stalks

Combine the tomato juice, onion, and garlic in a large pitcher. Cut a lengthwise slit in the jalapeño and add it to the tomato juice. Put the pitcher in the fridge and allow the flavors to infuse for at least a few hours, or as long as overnight.

To serve, stir in the remaining ingredients. Pour into tall glasses filled with ice, and garnish with the pickled okra and/or any of the other vegetables that you like.

agua fresca

Perfect when serving spicy Mexican food, it's delicious as is or spiked with tequila. Use just one kind of fruit—don't mix them! A colorful array of different batches of this drink made from all kinds of fresh fruit and served in clear glass pitchers is a beautiful display for a party.

4 cups (670 g) chopped fresh fruit, such as cantaloupe, honeydew melon, watermelon, or pineapple

3 tablespoons sugar

2 cups (480 mL) water

Juice of 1 lime

Combine the fruit, sugar, 1 cup (240 mL) of the water, and the lime juice in a blender and blend until smooth. Pour through a fine-mesh sieve into a pitcher, using a rubber spatula or wooden spoon to help push all the liquid through the sieve; discard the fruit pulp. Add the remaining 1 cup (240 mL) water and stir to combine. Chill in the refrigerator until ready to serve.

cape cod and collins jiggle shots

makes 32 (2-ounce/60 ml) shots

Yes, these jiggly "shots" are usually the domain of bars in college-town USA, but those are made from neon powdered Jell-O. Instead, we take a couple of classic cocktails and jiggle them up in a nod to college-party fun.

1¼ cups (300 mL) water

1 cup (200 g) sugar

1½ cups (360 mL) lemonade

1½ cups (360 mL) pure cranberry juice (no sugar added)

2 envelopes (4½ teaspoons/14 g) unflavored gelatin

2 cups (16 ounces/480 mL) vodka

Juice of 1 lemon

32 (3-ounce/90 mL) disposable plastic cups

Combine the water and sugar in a small saucepan. Bring to a boil, stirring until the sugar is dissolved. Keep warm, but don't let too much liquid evaporate.

Put the lemonade and cranberry juice in separate medium heatproof bowls and sprinkle 1 envelope

(2¼ teaspoons/7 g) of gelatin over each. Let stand until the gelatin softens, about 5 minutes.

Pour 1 cup (240 mL) of the hot simple syrup into the lemonade and stir until the gelatin is dissolved. Pour the remaining simple syrup into the cranberry juice and stir until the gelatin is dissolved. Add 1 cup (240 mL) of the vodka to each bowl and stir to combine. Stir the lemon juice into the lemonade mixture.

Place the plastic cups on a rimmed baking sheet. Divide the juices evenly among them. Cover with plastic wrap and refrigerate until set, at least 8 hours. The shots can be stored, covered, in the refrigerator for up to 1 week.

scotchie citrus punch

This unique cocktail turns to the spice cabinet and fruit and vegetable larder for inspiration. Made with local Jamaican allspice, citrus, and hot Scotch bonnets, it is warm and fruity with a kick to match an action-packed game.

1 cup (225 g) natural sugar, less if no unsweetened citrus such as lime is used

1 cup (240 mL) freshly squeezed citrus juice (grapefruit, orange, lime or any combo that isn't too sweet)

1 tablespoon fresh ginger, peeled and thinly sliced

2 whole Scotch bonnet or habanero chiles

8 whole allspice

Ice

Appleton Estate Jamaican rum

Club soda

Slices of fresh lime

Combine the sugar, citrus juice, ginger, chiles, and allspice in a small pan and bring to a boil. Cool and strain the mixture. Fill 6 glasses with ice. Fill each glass halfway with the citrus mixture, add 1 shot of rum each, top with club soda, and stir. Garnish with a slice of lime and serve.

To serve 30 guests, here are the quantities:

8 cups (1.6 kg) sugar • 20 cups (4.7 L) citrus juice • 20 tablespoons (240 g) sliced fresh ginger • 19 whole Scotch bonnet chiles • Scant ¼ cup (20 g) whole allspice • One 1.5-liter bottle (or two 750-milliliter bottles) rum • 2 liters club soda

When making a large batch, store the punch mix without club soda, adding the fizzy stuff only when ready to serve.

INDEX

Copyright © 2009, 2013, 2016, 2019 by Lucinda Scala Quinn

Back cover photographs and photographs on pages 15, 16, 21, 25, 30, 33, 35, 39, 41, 42, 47, 57, 69, 76, 79, 94, 101, 104, 107, 109 copyright © 2013, 2016 by Jonathan Lovekin

Photographs on pages 6, 9, 12, 26, 50, 53, 67, 85, 91, 97 copyright © 2009 by Mikkel Vang

All rights reserved. No portion of this book may be reproduced—mechanically, electronically, or by any other means, including photocopying—without written permission of the publisher.

Library of Congress Cataloging-in-Publication Data is on file.

ISBN 978-1-57965-935-6

Cover and book design adapted from Jennifer S. Muller and Erica Heitman-Ford

Front cover photograph by Lauren Volo

Artisan books are available at special discounts when purchased in bulk for premiums and sales promotions as well as for fund-raising or educational use. Special editions or book excerpts also can be created to specification. For details, contact the Special Sales Director at the address below, or send an e-mail to specialmarkets@workman.com.

For speaking engagements, contact speakersbureau@workman.com.

Published by Artisan
A division of Workman Publishing Co., Inc.
225 Varick Street
New York, NY 10014-4381
artisanbooks.com

Artisan is a registered trademark of Workman Publishing Co., Inc.

This book has been adapted from *Mad Hungry: Feeding Men and Boys* (Artisan, 2009), *Mad Hungry Cravings* (Artisan, 2013), and *Mad Hungry Family* (Artisan, 2016).

Published simultaneously in Canada by Thomas Allen & Son, Limited

Printed in China

First printing, July 2019

10 9 8 7 6 5 4 3 2 1